Seeds of Struggle
Songs of Hope

Poetry of emerging youth y sus maestros del movimiento

EL CENTRO DE LA RAZA

Edited by raúlrsalinas and Jennifer Shen

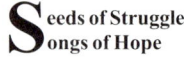

Seeds of Struggle
Songs of Hope

EL CENTRO DE LA RAZA

ISBN: 0-9633275-2-6
Library of Congress Catalog Card Number: 97-78435

Printed in the United States of America

For Information Write:

El Centro de la Raza
2524 16th Avenue South
Seattle, Washington 98144
Phone: (206) 329-9442
Fax: (206) 329-0786
elcentro@elcentro.org
www.elcentro.org

Other works from El Centro de la Raza:

Anglesey, Zoë, ed. *Word Up*. Seattle: El Centro de la Raza, 1992.

Maestas, Roberto and B.E. Johansen. *Nicaraguan Autonomy and the Lessons of the North American Indian Experience*. Presented at the "Conference on Autonomy for Atlantic Coast Provinces," Managua, Nicaragua, 1986.

Maestas, Roberto and B.E. Johansen. *El Pueblo: The Gallegos Family's American Journey, 1503-1980*. New York: Monthly Review Press, 1983. Mexico City: Fondo de Cultura y Económica, 1987.

Maestas, Roberto and B.E. Johansen. *Washington's Latino Community*. Seattle: Washington Commission for the Humanities, 1980.

Maestas, Roberto and B.E. Johansen. *Wasi'chu: The Continuing Indian Wars*. New York: Monthly Review Press, 1979. Mexico City: Fondo de Cultura y Económica, 1982.

Acknowledgments

We are grateful for permission to include in *Seeds of Struggle/Songs of Hope* the following:

"Glass," "Immigrant's Voice," and "Reform" by Naomi Ayala, originally published in *Wild Animals on the Moon* (Curbstone Press, 1997).

"The Barrio Artist/Teacher" and sketches: "Cholos," "La Joda y La Lucha Continue," and "Mother Earth" by José Montoya, originally published in *Information: 20 Years of Joda* (Chusma House Publications, 1992).

"Short Rap with Che," "About Invasion and Conquest," and "On the Police Murder of Jonathan Rodney" by raúlrsalinas, originally published in *East of the Freeway* (Red Salmon Press, Austin, Texas, 1995).

Special thanks to master artist Alfredo Arreguín who in his own words describes the significance of his painting titled "General Zapata": "Emiliano Zapata is the foremost symbol in Mexico of the people and the land. Whether we own it or work it, the land is the essence of life. Like Zapata, El Centro de la Raza grew out of the struggle for land for our people. Zapata exemplifies compassion and the struggle for justice and dignity, so it is a fitting image for El Centro de la Raza whose commitment to justice for farmworkers is in keeping with this spirit."

EL CENTRO DE LA RAZA

Summer Youth Leadership Institute Director:
Estela Ortega
Summer Youth Leadership Institute Coordinators:
Sara Sandoval
raúlrsalinas
Summer Youth Leadership Institute Anthology Editors:
raúlrsalinas
Jennifer Shen
Summer Youth Leadership Institute Artists in Residence:
Naomi Ayala
José Montoya
Lourdes Pérez
raúlrsalinas
Danny Desiga
Ricardo Favela
Fast Eddy Salas
Martin Luther King Class Teacher:
Delia González
Poetry Facilitator and Lino-cut Teacher:
Hap Bockelie
Program Blessing:
Steve Old Coyote
Special Presenter:
Jim Page
Book Design and Desktop Publishing:
Jennifer Shen
Final Pre-press Layout and Editing
Alexis Meyners
Richard Amerman
Mark Kines
Photography and Computers:
Roberta Lopez
Summer Youth Leadership Institute Interpreter:
Debbie Harris
Cover Art:
Alfredo Arreguín. "General Zapata", 1997.
(52" x 42" oil on canvas).
Cover Design:
Y Design
Technology Systems Coordinator:
Richard Amerman
Computer Assistant:
Gabriel González
Special Thanks to:
Department of Community, Trade and Economic Development
Princeton University Student Volunteers Council Summer Service Internship
Program
Seattle Arts Commission
Summer Youth Employment Program City of Seattle
The Seattle Times

We would also like to thank everyone at El Centro de la Raza for their
involvement and support of the Summer Youth Leadership Institute.

This book was designed and produced using Adobe Pagemaker® 6.5, Adobe
Photoshop® 4.0, and Paint Shop Pro® 4.12 on a Pentium® 90 PC. It was typeset in
Book Antiqua and Times New Roman.

DEDICATION

On our 25th anniversary, it is with great honor that El Centro de la Raza dedicates this book to the hard-working Farm Workers who toil in the fields daily to bring food to our tables. We celebrate our Farm Worker heritage and history proudly, and we support the Farm Workers in their noble struggle for equality, justice, dignity, and freedom. Compañeros, estamos con ustedes en la lucha.

Seattle, 1997

INTRODUCTION

In 1972, the burning social issues of our nation: educational inequity, economic discrimination, racial injustice, sexual repression and inner-city police violence— coupled with the aftermath of the Vietnam War, weighed heavily upon most people of this land. One direct result of these conditions, in Seattle Washington, was the occupation of an abandoned school building in the Beacon Hill neighborhood. Based in the Chicano/Latino community, among people who understood the necessity for social change, struggle and resistance, a dedicated, grass-roots organization was created within the American Civil Rights Movement. "...Y El Centro de la Raza became a REALITY!"

Since its inception, one of El Centro de la Raza's main objectives has been the development and empowerment of community members to advocate for positive social change. However, not much would have been accomplished to date, had we not acknowledged youth as our most valuable resource, or learned the important lesson that community is impossible without communication. So it is not a coincidence that at the heart of El Centro de la Raza's organizational logo, is the ancient Maya/Mexica symbol for communication, a glyph stemming from the open mouth of an indigenous person. This is a conscious *reconocimiento* of the ancestral belief that communication was an essential human activity. And that communication at its highest level of development is, simply, poetry.

It is also no coincidence that poetry is loved and developed in lands that have been subjected to the most vicious exploitation. When oppression becomes so unbearable to a people, poetry, among other forms of expression, flows and gushes forth, as part of the human spirit's rebel scream against injustice. Therefore, poetry too, was created by the people toiling to keep body/mind/soul intact in the cotton fields, banana plantations, gold mines, steel mills, shanty towns, migrant camps, ghettos, barrios, docks, sweatshops and chain gangs of this world. But "poetry" has too long been cloaked in so much elitism... and mysticism, that to many it is something intangible, unpalatable and inaccessible.

Poetry
has to be
the love that
cuts the ties that
bind the tongue.

The above poem, which is based on the application of poetry as an agent of change in people's lives, makes no bones about it; Poetry IS love! Not only that, it is love that <u>can cut</u>! That's some kind of love. And it has to be, because the ties that bind our tongues, like the chains that fetter our bodies are of the toughest, most brutal ilk... And one response to that must be the collective voice of social protest. Who has not seen (or been one of) our sullen youth hanging out on the street, expressing themselves (ourselves) through physical violence; or sitting in the back of the class, only acknowledging those around them in sheer, utter silence? We must impress upon these, and all youth, that community is vital to a just and sane society and to the overall protection of our sacred Mother Earth.

In that regard, El Centro de la Raza has also become a nurturing school for community leaders and... poets. For the past three years, El Centro has sponsored and hosted the Hope for Youth Summer Leadership Conference, which brings youth together with nationally known writers and performance artists. These cultural workers, whose work is youth-oriented, conduct classes and facilitate workshops combining the teachings of Dr. Martin Luther King's political and theological works, histories of communities of color, grassroots organizing, cultural exchanges, anger-management/conflict resolution and leadership through poetry, that is... communication. This year was no exception, as the students worked with: poet/activists Naomi Ayala and raúlrsalinas, master muralist/poet José Montoya of the Royal Chicano Air Force and singer/songwriter Lourdes Pérez -- hence this anthology.

Among the many gifts we wish to share on this 25th anniversary of our humble, but firm and resolute existence, is this anthology. Once again, daring to "cut the ties that bind"; for the unbound tongues of our young people have much to relate to us. LISTEN!

Hap Bockelie and raúlrsalinas
Seattle 1997

CONTENTS

ALEX ACOSTA

My name is Alex Acosta. I was born in Bronx, New York, on October 25, 1982. I am a very independent person. I am a true PUERTO-RIQUEÑO and I am "proud of it." I will never let my people down nor would they take me down. I love my beautiful Island with all my heart and will never sell out. I say sell out because my people and your people have been brainwashed by the "EVIL people in power" who have tried to tear our people apart. I will always stand my ground because I love my people.

I AM

I am me,
I am known as a G
not as a gangsta ,
but as that man that will spank ya
I am coo,
but I'm for sure not a foo
I am curious,
and that's why I'm mysterious
I am a writer,
and my styles are gettin' tighter
I got some styles of fame,
and that's why people know my name
I am a sportsman ,
and my basketball skills are like Michael Jordan's
my baseball skills are dope,
and that's why scouts will scope.
I am proud,
and for that I am loud
I am PUERTO RICAN,
and that is why I am speakin'

"GUNS"

Guns, oh guns, why are they alive,
people are dying and their mothers will cry.

Guns, oh guns, why must they live,
one silver or gold bullet is all that they give.

Guns, oh guns, will they let you survive,
no, they won't, they are just a lie.

When will we put an end to this really cruel crime,
while all of our people are trying to survive.

Guns, oh guns, when will they go away,
when they put a bullet in wrong, and their family member
pays.

Guns, guns... !!BANG!!BANG!!

TODAY

Today I saw the boy listen to the other boy to ride the bike,

Today I saw the owner of the bike,

Today I found out the bike was stolen,

Today I heard him tell me "RUN,"

Today I "RAN,"

Today the cop knocked on the door,

Today the river inside me was flowing loosely,

Today I let loose,

Today I became "FREE."

MY ISLAND

My Island, my island,
what a wonderful place,
a place where I can go and share
this beautiful space.

A place of love,
from high above
my island, my island,
my heart pumps for your love.

The sound of the wind
breezing through the air,
the smell of chuletas
arroz con habichuelas
makes my hunger be aware.

Umm! The smell, umm! The feel
makes me shiver inside
the love for my island
I know will never DIE!

BRENDA ADAMS

My name is Brenda Adams Castañeda. I'm 15 years old. I was born in Seattle, Washington, raised in L.A. My mom is Nora Elena Castañeda, born in Medellín, Colombia. My dad is Keith Adams; he is Native American. My plans for the future are to graduate from high school, go to college, and get a degree as a designer. I would like to be an actress and singer. Aside from that, I would also like to get married and have four kids. I'm a Cancer, so I'm really into my family.

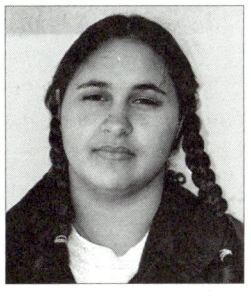

NO LLORES MAS MI'JA

No puedo moverme
can't run
ni puedo gritar
nomas puedo esperar
que se termine todo
pero sé que nunca va a parar.
Lagrimas caen de mis ojos
no sé porque
or maybe I do
but don't want to remember
I feel as if my heart is bleeding
the pain grows stronger
"no llores mas mi'ja
todo va a estar bien,"
are the last words I hear.

LA VIDA NUESTRA

Life begins when you are conceived
Ends in a matter of seconds.
I hear laughter.
Are they laughing 'cause they're happy?
No, they're just high and drunk,
laughing at everything.
Babies crying 'cause mom is high.
When they're off the high,
guns go off,
anger is turned into hatred.
That's how it goes en los barrios de nuestra gente.
Been there,
done that.
Gente mía,
why do that to your familia?

COLOMBIANA

Colombian is what I am.
Brown is the color of my people.
Proud is what we are.
Vida es lo que traemos.
Siempre estaremos al lado
de nuestra familia.
Juntos porque somos
iguales, como seres humanos.
Don't forget that.

LOVE

There are two types of love:
love between two people;
the love between family and friends.
Love can be expressed in different ways.
Disappointment
Pain
Revenge
Struggle
Joy
Happiness

NAOMI AYALA
Artist in Residence

Naomi Ayala migrated from Puerto Rico as an adolescent in the late 1970s and settled in New Haven where she lives and works today as an arts administrator and a poet-in-schools. She has been anthologized in *In Creative Resistance: Puerto Rican Women Writers in the U.S.* Her first collection of poetry, *Wild Animals on the Moon*, was released by Curbstone Press in the spring of 1997.

GLASS

-- for Gayle Hall, activist, poet,
single parent of seven and adoptive mother of one.

I am a women learning to be free
Every day I weep
drawing chipped glass
from my calloused feet

Papi said vases can be glued & bowls & figurines
when I was small
My brother says *now, ain't no use holding*
on to broken things
My lover says *let me give you kisses*

My history is glass I walk on
with my soul on fire
I am a women learning to be free
My history pours hard over my shoulder
blows like a typhoon

and I become thunder in the dark
and my eyes tell no lies
they say *free me* when I talk every day

I weep drawing chipped glass
from my calloused feet
gathering all the pieces afterwards

IMMIGRANT'S VOICE

I heard an immigrant's voice.
It rubbed the walls of downtown
buildings clean,
wiped the glass of steamy truckstop
windows with its breath
& o.d.'d on caffeine
& cigarettes, dawns before work.

It cleared a fog in January
with its whistle in its jeans,
climbed the flag poles on the Green & shouted,
itself a mast recited
from the dollar
e pluribus unum e pluribus unum.

It prayed in front of the gates
of Union Trust,
climbed city hall steps -- kneecaps to concrete
during unemployment --
& asked the mayor, please, a shot of whiskey
or dope, or a dollar, a mighty dollar.

It cut open its forearm six inches
at his machine operator's job
cutting steel --
his words deep-blue-purple
but he had to be grateful,
he had to be grateful for the work.

It pounded on its lover's breast,
this voice
demanding *where* is the dream?
Where *is* the dream?

It broke into tears at public urinals
& spit on statues on the way home
until sweat poured
from the contour
of their histories.

It gargled the news
nights after suppertime
& crawled shivering into its sleep
What sleep there could be.
What dreams.

REFORM

You know we have always been poor,
always been suspect, the ragwater cocktail
of their bad dreams. And, Rebecca, again they say
they want us to be free. This and that
stuff of salvation by handout assistance.
They want yet for us another freedom of *progress
in self-sufficiency* while they fingerprint
our hands for food. And, nobody's talking up
our case rationally enough, they say.
Yet these are the times of organized lunacy --
though no one fingerprints them for our tears.
No one fingerprints them for our hunger.
José, where could I be now? Ten miles east
of a hot plate of food? Frankie, what more
can they do? Bodyslam us where your body lay
in the street till we bleed again through you?
How to scratch the eyes out
of the face of hunger's monster, María,
when you're too weak to be clear, drowning
slow death by drowning in their filth?
Is it like cooking for eight children?
Half yours, half not your own?
Is it easier than not having enough?
Is it harder than the future?
How will we kick back out of this one?
Who will come for us, Miguel,
if we are too broken?
The sign of the cross here's
been walking gunshyless & believing
tomorrow might be the same
as we rub the rosary beads of employment
listings so they may yield.
Anything resembling walls will have to
suffice for a house. Even the coffin of our children's
time-bombed lives the moment they leave our wombs.
And praying's done me personally so much
good, now I bask in the luminosity
of neon, in this rainbow-colored song,
believe one day he too might come for me
like the god of employment -- off his information super highway
shortcut with the sanctity
of city dump angels beating
their aluminum wings

LOVE

When we struggle together to understand
we uncover and overcome
fear of losing
courage and confidence.
Curious
about what's going to happen,
we gain courage
to understand the truth
which entails sacrifice --
sweat, blood
cold and warm.
But victory
is sweet as whipcream
on a cinnamon bun
covered with chocolate
and strawberries.
All the injustices
that are happening right now --
an eye for an eye --
we'll deal with to go
to "the biggest dance of the year."

HAP BOCKELIE

Like you, I came into this life choiceless. I was what I was, a working class baby with blue eyes, *huevitos*, and U.S. citizenship. In 1956, no one in my town could tell me what that meant: a cog in the wheel of a well-oiled machine, designed to take and stamp brown people into coins to fill the pockets of the white guys who own the machine. I'm still an unhappy cog, but lately I've gotten out of alignment, squeaking out a poem every so often.

WATSONVILLE '97

Picnicing
America sinking white
Teeth deep into
Sweet
Red pulp it
Didn't want to know
Is campesino
Blood
Clotting in-between
Belgian waffle and whipped cream.

DO IT

Inside any
exit-locked
IN-DONE-sian
sweat-shop
nike swoosh =
nazi swastika
nothing less
in Seattle
Nike Town
glitzy-slick
light sound
seamless multi-
ethnic salespeople
tanning booth clientele
set the style
to be seen in casual
athletic american cool
Just Do It
at 10 p.m.
on Mickey D's
assembly line
Just Do It
in dusty Mattawa
migrant camps
Just Do It
behind the till
at 7-11
Just Do It
in the un
employ
ment line
JUST DO IT!!!

CANCIONES DE DON JESÚS

Adjusting
her bathing suit
the guests had gone
"Dawn Hay-soos, why
do the songs you sing always
contain so much pain?"
He didn't say
"estás
equivocada."
He said, "Señora
my guitar
strung with barbed wire
comes from the border."

TRUE LOVE

She accused him
of mountains
He came back with
accusations of his own
Sky! Cloud! Kisses blown!
Soon plateaus, swallows
the aydilla* of the tortilla
blue whales, begonias, and
2nd hand sales
flew madly between them
Guilty as coyotes
they snuggled
in blame.

*aydilla: Spanglish spelling of idea.

MARIT BOCKELIE

My name is Marit Bockelie. I've spent sixteen years of my life growing up in the Pacific Northwest. It is very beautiful here, but like anywhere in the United States, it is full of people who have been controlled, sheltered from reality, and cut off from the people of the rest of the world. During the remainder of my years on earth I will work to help breakdown these barriers between my people of this planet.

I WILL BLOOM

you say you want to know
you say you need to know
the other side of me
you say you want to know

but to show this to you
but to share me with you
would mean bridging the gap
to show this to you

you want to meet that girl
you want the girl inside
I need to open up
for you to meet that girl

could I be that grounded
could I be connected
to the both of me strong
to the two of me strong

I have kept the gap wide
and you at just one end
to keep the pain from me
to keep the pain from me

keep picking at my brain
keep prying at my soul
if you will force me open
I will bloom in your hands

THE CLOWN AND THE CLOWNFISH

What if?
    And what if you do?
What if you do know the meaning of life
Sit,
with hands growing from keyboard growing from plastic
Stare lovingly
at the screen through which you see the world
"No" you tell me with that computerized voice box

No, the meaning of life is not about the indescribable
The unmeasureable notions of love
About the reasonings behind orange anemones
of tentacle after tentacle
after reach towards optical beauty
Clown Fish it will never see

No, the meaning of life is not that
It's not the sound that stars make
when they call to the sea
When night allows the scales allows the water
allows stretch into a kiss
Not the reflection of this in an island child

I admit wholeheartedly that it could not be any of this
The meaning of life could not
be found in human similarity to the sea
No, it's definitely not that, it must be
found some where between cyber circuits
and the intense blockade you've raised
against the world

DEATH

Death will be lucky if he gets me first
I will have a lot to offer, you know
He's probably watching right now
Death, is most likely, in fact, watching me right now

And, boy is he jealous
His wife could not compare
He could kill for brown eyes this round
and mango skin this deep

He sits quietly, tapping a finger
to the beat of my breath
in and out and In and Out and steady
as the lifebeat moving my people

He wants to crawl deep into my soul
and live as part of my life
to give up hellfire and paradise
and know love this well

Yes, Death is in love with me
At night my soul is swept away into the darkness
so he can dance to my rhythm
And I am free to come home

Death's arms long to hold me
listen and breath me
Let each stand and eyelash
Run over his tongue when I'm not looking

…Death is in love with me
But I HAVE TOO MUCH TO DO
And when *he's* not looking
I'm gonna eat him
                    Alive!

CUBA

A word with no literal meaning
(A place where literature thrives
on the island and at the mention of her name)
But her history
goes on being of the immense human heart
Even from thousands of miles away
my pen forces me in anticipation
in excitement to learn all I can
I wait to leave and
the sky is quietly changing
an example of transformed non-conformism
somewhere exactly between blue and heaven
reflecting Caribbean water
Soon I'll be there
Where palms are as strong as the people
We are all preparing.

MARTHA CASTAÑEDA

I was born in Los Angeles, California, on September 17, 1982. My father and my mother are both from Medellín, Colombia. I like playing volleyball, basketball, and softball. I go to Chief Sealth High School and I am in the tenth grade. I want to go to college. Then, when I accomplish what I put myself to do, I'll make my family. The reason I wouldn't make my family sooner is because I want my children to have everything. I don't want them to come to and suffer in this world.

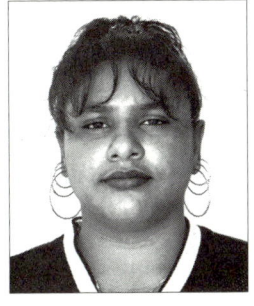

SPEAK OUT

In this world there's so much violence,
so much unfairness.
There's so many people that like it.
There's ones that don't.
The ones that do, they don't talk,
but there's so much to say.
Tell me!
TELL ME WHY!!
Why is it that when you see
something that you don't like,
you act like a ANVIL?
You don't say anything
or do anything.
You let them lead
you let them do what they want
NO you are wrong!
You suppose you are right, but I don't think so.
What are you afraid of ?
What they'll say,
Or What?
Did you run out of excuses?
Say what you feel
Or else you're going to be a part of the problem.
So please be a part of the solution!!!

I LOVE YOU

This is no occasion
that I'll let you know
Just showing you some passion
because I love you

I think about you everyday
and the things you say and do
You thrill my heart in every way
and thats why I love you

To me, you are my everything
and you mean a whole lot to me
you do the sweetest things
a guy could ever do.

You know for you I'll do anything
a girl could possibly do
you know to you my heart belongs
and never will I let you go.

I promise you to try my best
to be true, as true can be
I'm hoping that I'll pass the test
so my heart will be free.

I'm hoping things will go alright
for both, you and me
we can surely make our future bright
you just wait and see.

But dear, you must keep loving me
and never let me go
I want you I need you
because I love you so.

COLOMBIAN PRIDE

I am Colombian
-n-
I am brown
-n-
proud like a rose opening with the sun rise
Mi vida es mi familia
y
siempre seremos unidos
like a rose in a rose garden como los pétalos
que todos son iguales.
A mi familia yo los quiero con todo mi corazón.

JOSÉ DÍAZ

I was born in Pasco, Washington, on February 4, 1981. I have two brothers and two sisters. Even though I currently live in Western Washington, I plan to move back to Pasco after the conference is over. I realize that people make mistakes in life, but the way I see it is that you learn from your mistakes. When I was younger I thought about taking the short-cut through. Now I know that's not good at all. I'd rather take the long way because it's the right way to success.

SOMEBODY

There's someone in your life
that really means a lot to you.
Even though you don't realize that
when you're at a certain point in life.
But after years have passed by,
you will finally notice.

THE SCREW

I use to be part of a hinge,
but I screwed myself out.
After a while you realize you need a hinge to be cared by.
But now I don't have a hinge.
I'm just a free screw from all the hinges on the door.

STRANGER

I remember the stranger came to my farm.
He told me he needed help,
that he had to come out of his hole
to come up and feel good.
So I loaned the stranger a white goat.
The stranger went out and loaned it to other strangers.
But he never came back around or said anything.
He thought I forgot about the goat that I loaned him.
The stranger came back when he needed more goats.
But I told him that I had no more goats on my farm,
even though I had goats on my farm.
He knew it too.
But he knew that he'd just lost
his credit.

ENRIQUE GONZÁLEZ

My name is Enrique González. I'm 15 years old and a sophomore at Renton High School. I was born December 5, 1981 at Northwest Hospital in Seattle. My parents are both from Mexico. My father is from Chihuahua and my mother is from Guanajuato. I have one sister and one brother. I enjoy running, playing the saxophone, doing martial arts, and writing. I have been involved with El Centro de la Raza since I was born. My life is currently under construction, so I have much more to accomplish.

POISONOUS WATER AT SCHOOL

The mic is on, the lights are lit, the podium set,
Every seed is listening.
The poisonous water pours upon the them.
Seeds do not know what life is about.
Listening like thirsty souls.
The hose speaks like a deceiving serpent,
strengthening the smoking, choking weeds.
Contaminating, and robbing our
seedlings,
of the truth that rightfully belongs to them.
They yearn to break through the earth.
Every flower strives to reach the light.
I am a filter for lies.
The eradicator of deception.
Preying upon propaganda,
and feeding on the
truth.

MY TIME HAS COME

My time has come young man,
time to rest.
Time to vegetate,
shrivel up and die.
What do you speak of
old one?
Why do you summon the
Angel of death?
Your selfishness will be
your demise.
You have activated your
self-destruction mode.
I must confess,
I do not wish to
self-terminate.
My faith remains with the creator,
that when my time comes
I'll be ready.
The moment we are born,
we are one step closer to death.
So don't waste your time
on this limited offer.
A single shot at fulfilling
the unknown purpose,
carried out the moment we die.
So I ask you old one,
Why grieve over what is
destined to happen?
Without death there is no life.
Death is a plus,
a promotion
toward immortality.

YOU LIE

You lie to me,
with a huge smirk
on your face,
you try to rob
me of the truth.
My truth is guarded
by the alarm of my
heart.
I am aware of your
flaw.
The dragon that you daily
struggle to slay.
We are together in the fight
against our own dragons.

THE DREAM OF LIFE

The book is read, so we can
write the letter.
Related by ink to the pen,
the pencil finishes the drawing.
Life is added by colors,
giving drama and beauty to plants.
Producing wood for the
foundation of our house,
then,
"I wake up."

THE BROKEN SHACKLES

I used to be a hard-working horse,
one who worried about what others thought,
pulled in the direction I didn't want.
Not pleasing myself,
only others.
Earning recognition
without being recognized.
I am now a screaming falcon,
liberated from the shackles of expectation,
and setting my
own navigational flight path.

PATRICIA HERNÁNDEZ

Mi nombre es Patricia Hernández. A mí me gusta escribir poemas. Yo soy de Mexico, de una ciudad llamada Guanajuato. Hace poco que llegué a los Estados Unidos, por eso todavía no puedo escribir en inglés. Espero que entiendan español para que lean mis poemas. Yo no soy muy buena para escribir poemas pero los hice con todo mi cariño.

EL AMOR

El amor es algo muy profundo.
Es algo que solamente algunas personas tienen, ese don de amar de verdad.
Pero yo creo que todas las personas deben amar, por que las que no aman,
siempre están muy tristes y amargadas.
En cambio, una persona que está enamorada siempre esta muy féliz y sonriente por que Dios nos amó y perdonó a los que le hicieron daño.
Por eso nosotros debemos perdonar para ser felices, por que dicen que el que no perdona, Dios no lo perdona.
Así como Dios le dijo a su padre "Dios mío, perdónalos por que no saben lo que hacen."
Están ciegos del corazón. Por eso como Dios, nosotros debemos perdonar a los que nos hacen daño o algún día nos hicieron algún mal.

A BOOK

The drawings are very pretty
like flowers of many colors
pretty like homes with windows
to look outside
with very big plants.

UN LIBRO

Los dibujos son muy bonitos
como flores de muchos colores
bonitos como casas con ventanas
para ver hacia afuera
con plantas muy grandes.

LA CIUDAD

Esta ciudad es muy bonita
y muy grande.
Pero nunca se compara
con mi querido México.
México para mi es mucho.
Por que yo allí nací.
Por que allá tengo mi amiga,
que es como mi hermana.
Por que allá tengo familia
como mis tíos
mis tías
sobrinos
amigas
amigos
y una hermana.
Yo espero algún día poder volver
a verla
para estar juntas otra vez.
Para ser muy felices,
es mi deseo
es lo que yo espero.

MEXICO

México, México, donde estarás. Mi querido México,
quien se retira de su tierra no la olvida porque
todos queremos el lugar donde nacimos.
México, te veo en mi mente y en mi corazón.
Cuando veo el cielo te recuerdo,
cuando veo las estrellas y la luna te recuerdo,
Siempre te recordaré.
Sobre todo,
a las personas que están lejos de mí.

ALEJANDRO BAUTISTA MAGAÑA

Mi nombre es Alejandro Bautista Magaña. I was born in Guadalajara, Jalisco, tierra de Aztlán. I am 18 years old, a community builder, and a *Mechista*. Seattle confronted me at 3 years of age when my mom and dad decided to move to this city for survival purposes. Our family of 3 did not understand English nor the capitalist city life of Seattle. The Mexican tradition of Raza and Familia is one that I embrace and share with the people of this planet. This is just a hint of my life. I invite you to get to know me better.

LETRAS

Xtra small peach
with a mango flavor
so watery
it's wet
con sal y limón combined with salsa
in a hypnotic movement
just like wind hitting the palm tree sideways
monopolizing the shade of the natural color of the coco
which in time
you might be destined
if you do not know
to be hispanicized.

THE ACCUSED

"Just another Mexican"
was what I figured
when you accused me of tire marking your walls
and using your position as manager
to act like the insensitive mero mero.
In broad daylight,
life was evolving
and the Berlin Wall stood in our parking lot
as though it was a national landmark.
I explained, your ignorance shallows your truth.
When rage took you over
truth and courage nurtured my soul
and gave me the strength
to understand the world in your eyes.

STRENGTH

Pride Brown,
Red Wine,
Black Richness,
It happens when my culture is nurtured.
It makes me feel like a bull charging at the bullfighter.
Humility,
Knowledge,
Strategy,
I have Strength!

ELISA MIRANDA

My name is Elisa María Miranda. I was born May 18, 1981 in Tri-Cities, WA. My mother's side of the family comes from Guanajuato, Mexico and my dad's side from San Luís Potosí, Mexico. My parents were both migrant Farm Workers. My family is very active in the Farm Workers' struggle. I have been with El Centro de la Raza for seven years, currently as a youth intern, organizing and recruiting for its youth programs. I am a published poet and have done public speaking.

MY SELF-LOVE

Dreams drip on my cultivating mind
wanting to visit the great madness
of this world.
Rise above my comfort zone
and look at past histories
trying to effect new histories
my flourishing eyes know only what they see.
I don't want to imprison them
to one way of living
confined to one way of thinking.
My duty?
To celebrate life!
Every moment
every day
I am the compassion that my people have
tying me down to the truth.
I am both sides of the struggle
it's conflict grows roots in my chest
too close to my heart.
I am the Chicana
with a thousand cultures
which cannot be denied!

STAINED PICTURES

These images of poverty
of homemade corn tortillas
cooked on the closest thing
they have to a stove
hungry hijos
and busy mothers
with long dresses
that to many
may seem nothing more than a rag.
But to me
it is the dress of an
mechica princess.
Goddess
waiting
anticipating
running on the hot gravel
with bare feet
calming to the shadow of the sunlight
wanting to play
to let the summer
be your childhood memory
siempre mirando sus padres
bent over
crouching with pain
still moving on down the row.

The only protection
against the slave owner's unbearable heat
is a little white sombrero
the same sombrero of Pancho Villa
and the thousands
at the battle of Puebla.
Brown fists
raised up high
to faces
who are reveling in their ignorance
presenting the hands of those who built temples
that could never be built
lived
what could never be lived.
Now carrying broken wood
to warm the cowardly
and enslave the courageous
with a torn poncho
and a sad hat
he walks past riches
that belong to him
not being able to touch them
as descendants of historians
martyrs
mothers
we must ask
"How will we continue
this struggle that never began with us?"

REALITY IN A DREAM

Every breath I take
you are my faith.
Nights I sit alone
My mind in a clone
thinking of you everyday
hoping you'll come my way.
I pray every night
life will hold you tight,
I don't know what to do
Or how to hold and love you.
Your eyes have me in prison
giving me the reason to have risen
each morning
to every glory.
Silent pains without your kiss
you're the one I miss,
I will carry every burden you take
What I'm feeling isn't fake.
My life a song
with you I hope it to be long
everyday passing by
getting so strong.
The insomnia making me weak
so much I can barely speak
You my king
and me to be your queen.
Life without you is cruel
although you can be a stubborn mule
take what I am saying for real
and I'll be here.

HOPE, COURAGE, MY PEOPLE

I want to take my life back
and sacrifice it
to the masses of my people,
hoping they will endure me.

If I keep this small life
to myself
it will be hard to have the hope of a warm plate
of tortillas
y chile con carne.
It will be hard
to have the courage
of a candle embroidered with the body of my *virgen*.
It will be so hard.

But somehow I've gotten by
it may be
because I have seen
new born poets read
or it may be because I have listened
to the sweat of my father as it falls off his forehead.

JOSÉ MONTOYA
Artist in Residence

José Montoya was born in Escoboza, New Mexico. He was raised in Albuquerque, New Mexico and California. A multidisciplinary artist (poet, painter, writer and musician), José is a founding member of the Rebel Chicano Art Front, also know as the Royal Chicano Air Force, a group of artist and writers in Sacramento. He is currently a professor of art at Sacramento State University.

CHOLO

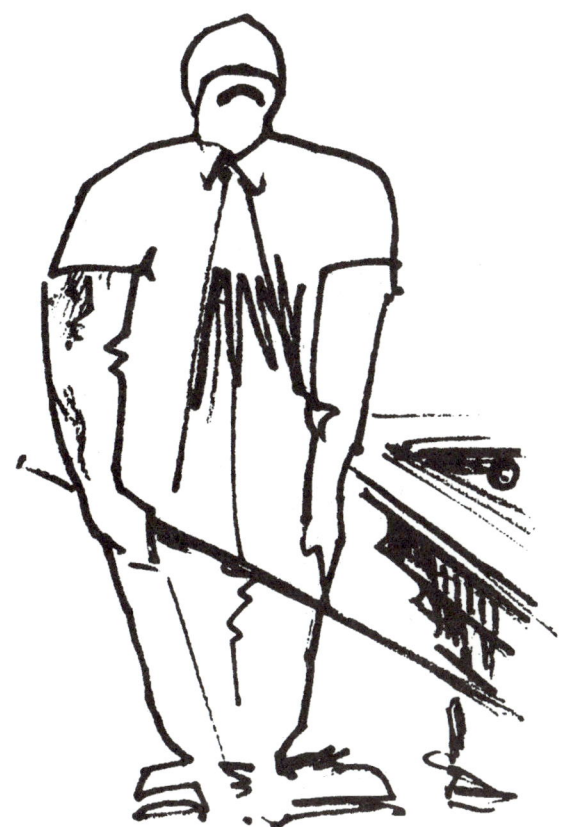

THE BARRIO ARTIST/TEACHER

Pa'los del RCAF

Because to create
Is to give life
The barrio artist/teacher
Commits acts of love...
And risks
Seeming selfish.

But

To look into
the eyes
Of a child
Discovering
The magic
Of color
Amidst squalor --

To see
A stone
Vato loco
Caressing
A ball of clay --

To discern
As wrinkled
Fingers forget

The pain of aging --

It has to be a
Selfless
Selfishness.

LA JODA Y LA LUCHA CONTINUE

MOTHER EARTH

LOURDES PÉREZ
Artist in Residence

Composing from the roots of Puerto Rico and the soul of *nueva trova*, Lourdes Pérez has a truly remarkable voice. She has toured the United States & Mexico and has performed with the famed Argentine singer, Mercedes Sosa. Lourdes is frequently commissioned to write special tributes and has received airplay in Italy, Australia and Taiwan. In 1994 she released her debut CD, <u>Recuérdate Por Mi</u>, and her latest work, <u>Vestigios</u>, is scheduled for release in November 1997.

FELIZ 25: AL CENTRO DE LA RAZA

Centro de La Raza
De la Raza Centro
Donde el movimiento
Construyó su casa
Tu historia, la masa
Que alimenta sueños
Dedicando empeños
a tí, su futuro,
Removiendo muros
Sin creerse el dueño.

Los grandes poderes
Quieren mutilarte
y un tercio quitarte
De lo que hoy tu eres
Hombres y Mujeres
De dedicación
y una tradición
Que es de pura lucha
tu dignidad es mucha
No hay comparación

¿Como han de quitar
a un ave su vuelo?
la lluvia del cielo
nunca ha de secar.
¿Como despintar
tus bellos murales?
grandes ideales
guardan sus colores
Ustedes son flores
y el pueblo lo sabe.

[Collective Décima with SYLI class:]

Hay que poner atención
la historia de nuestra gente
Quieren robar de repente
Don't you know this is our home
El Centro es nuestro cantón
Para seguir la nación
De conquistas y traiciones
We have truth in our canciones
You can't buy us out with fear
People shed tears for what is here
They gave us their corazones.

August 4, 1997

CANTARLES QUISIERA

Cantarles quisiera
Alex y Vinh Phan
quien es de Vietnam
y atrás no se queda
de esta compañera
reciban saludos
Rebecca, los duros
tiempos ya se irán
Patricia, que tal,
Elisa, saludos.

Recibe Angelina
versos y cantares
que aprendí en solares
y en varias colinas
mi isla es la mina
de la inspiración
Alex, desde el Bronx
conoce su historia
José, Enrique, es gloria cantar la canción

Raúl, Spider, hermanos
jóvenes poetas
futuros profetas
yo estrecho mi mano
suelo Borincano
me dió la poesía
tengo una alegría
en el corazón
les doy mi canción
y mi companía
junto con Annette
nuestra companía.

DESPEDIDA

A los estudiantes
Que vienen al centro
Yo tomo un momento
Para gracias darles
Quisiera expresarles
Te tengo un orgullo
Tu voz es capullo
Que abrirá mañana
Vistiendo de gala
A tí y a los tuyos

Yo soy la cantora
la puertorriqueña
y my alma isleña
Brilla como aurora
y si un día se asoman
tiempos tormentosos
Recuerden el gozo
De andar en la lucha
Háblenle al que escucha
Celebren lo hermoso

A Raúl y a Sara
Celebres maestros
Queremos con esto
Cerrar la cantada
Gracias por la espada
la herramienta buena
a verdad me suenan
Sus nobles palabras
Pues futuro labran
rompiendo cadenas
El future labran
rompiendo cadenas

VINH PHAN

My name is Vinh Phan. I was born on May 15, 1983, in Saigon, south of Vietnam. I went to Nguyen Viet Xuan Elementary School from first to fifth grade. I didn't finish fifth grade in that school because I had to move to America with my family. At first I felt very sad because I had to leave my relatives and especially my friends, but when I met my uncles, aunts, and cousins I felt a lot better. I've gone to Tops Elementary School, Mercer Middle School, and Hamilton Middle School.

TRANSFORMED

I used to be a very weak person.
I did not have the courage to fight my fear,
like speak in front of the public
and always get distracted by other things
like games, movies, and clothes.
But then a couple of weeks ago,
I went to a Summer Youth Leadership Institute class.
They taught me how to become more organized,
they also gave me more confidence.
Now I can speak in front of the public
Without getting distracted by other things.

SAD MEMORIES

Everyday I keep wondering
about the past and the present
of Vietnam where I lived.
Many things have happened,
but most of them brought suffering
to the people of Vietnam.
Life keeps getting harder everyday.
Parents have to work day and night,
twelve to sixteen hours a day
to support their own families.
But many people are worse
because they don't have jobs.
They have to go around the streets
to pick up bags and cans to sell
for money to pay for their meals.
But enough with these sad memories,
I only hope there'll be a better future.

'CAUSE I DON'T HAVE MONEY!

I am poor
'cause I don't have money
I am starved
'cause I don't have money
I'm not the same
'cause I don't have money
I lost my family
'cause I don't have money
I lost my home
'cause I don't have money
I lived on the street
'cause I don't have money
I'm a beggar
'cause I don't have money
I have no friends
'cause I don't have money
I have no education
'cause I don't have money
I committed crimes
'cause I don't have money
I went to jail
'cause I don't have money
My life is miserable
'cause I don't have money
Yours will be the same
If you don't have money.

BOREDOM

White, light blue, and purple.

It happens when someone talks to me for hours,

it makes me feel like I'm in prison.

Sleepy, tired, and dying.

BECKY PRENDEZ

My name is Rebecca Prendez. I am 14 years old and a student at Canyon Park Junior High School. I was born in Kirkland, raised in California and Bothell. I play fastpitch softball. I also take boxing and kickboxing. As for my future, all that I really want is happiness. It doesn't matter how much, or how little I have, just as long as I have my happiness. For now, I'm just trying to become less self-centered, and know that I can make a difference in this world.

YOU WOULDN'T, YOU WOULD

You wouldn't trade your drugs,
for some hugs.

You wouldn't stop all your fights,
you say there is just too much hype.

You wouldn't exchange your gun,
to go be a nun.

But wouldn't you trade your drugs,
if you knew it would just get you mugged?

Wouldn't you stop all your fights,
if you knew that you still had that might?

And wouldn't you exchange your gun,
if you knew it would save your son?

LITTLE STAR

You were the kind of friend I could depend on,
you would never be gone.

Through thick and thin,
you remained my best friend.
You stayed by my side, and held my head high whenever I
would cry.

I think of you day and night,
I pray that we can make things right.

I know you're a great person inside and out.
If only you would see how many people want to help you,
if only you would count.

Under the moon's shadow is where I lay,
trying to fix my life out of total dismay.

As I look up into the sky,
lonely tears fall from my eye.
 stare up into the stars, and I am reminded of you,
oh Lord, what am I to do?

The light that would shimmer and shine,
so bright it would show me the way.
You always knew what to do and exactly what to say.

I have to admit you were a little wild,
but your ways have changed for you're no longer a child.

So now you're on vacation, you my little star,
I hope to God I can find out where you are.

And since I cannot talk or see you anymore,
my heart is permanently sore.

I love your eyes, your smile, your laughter,
I even shared your tears,
but these memories are becoming smeared.

I will love you forever,
and I'll always mourn my
fallen star.

CRUSH

I look at you and wonder why,
as lonely tears fall from my eye.

You see, I have a crush on you,
what am I to do?

I am younger, this you'll see,
for us to have a love,
you have the power,
you hold the key.

I look at you with the utmost respect.
My little secret about you,
I've always kept.

When you look at me through your beautiful eyes,
do you only see my
childish cries?

Because of you, I'm seeing illusions,
because of you, my mind's full of confusion.

I want to be with you night and day,
but I know it can never be that way.

Your charm has pierced me like a dart,
and I want you to know
I'll always hold you in my heart.

RAÚL SALINAS
Artist in Residence

raúlrsalinas grew up in Austin, Texas, where he is currently living. He has worked extensively with the American Indian Movement, the International Indian Treaty Council, and the Prisoners' Rights Support Network. He is the author of three poetry collections: the chapbook *Viaje/Trip* (1973), and the books *Un Trip through the Mind Jail* (1980), and *East of the Freeway* (1995). He is now working on another volume of poetry, *Indio Trails: A Xicano Odyssey through Indian Country.*

SHORT RAP WITH CHE

i've never written you a poem
before because...
i felt others had said it
All.

Yet, striving to exemplify your life,
become
El Hombre Nuevo,
is to
Me
rendering
You
my
Ultimate Poem.

>   *-- austin*
>   *Día del Guerrillero Heroico*
>   *october 8, 1987*

ABOUT INVASION AND CONQUEST

*composed during the Quincentenary
Monopoem Literary Circle*

They came with disrespectful feet
trampling sacred soil
strangers lacking color,
as if unkissed by the Sun.
Bearing cutlass and cross,
grossly they stepped on the land
to be honored with gifting
as guests at the feast.
But greedy for gold
tobacco offerings were
considered "primitive"
then placed among the other
fruits ripe for plucking,
sucking Native resources
to be peddled in the marketplace
before the queen.
As the pillage and plunder continued,
a young Taíno asked: "Who will be left
to tell of what happened to us, Grandfather?"
An elder replies: "Among those who survive,
there will be poets to recount
that which happened to us."
Ay, cristóbal colón… ¡Y qué colón!
Long tail that left doors open
for the other clowns/ cortés and the boys
clumsily rattling of sabre and sword
lording over indio (sharing) customs
clad in tin costumes Metallica never would claim.

Maiming Warrior Women
stripping of the Chieftains
they proceeded to cut down our flowers,
tried to silence our songs

DIScovery in what god's name???
"Who will live to tell
of what happened to us, Grandmother?"
a young Mexica asked.
La Anciana responds: "Among the survivors
there will be poets, they will relate
 that which happened to us."
Six generations later, after the bison is (almost) gone,
ravaged Mother Earth, by force produces
matter that turns into bombs
belching poison taints the waters,
kills the plants, pollutes the skies--
contaminated communities
victims of toxic chemical wars.
And today, when 500 winters have passed,
among the survivors
are poets
sitting in circle
telling the story
of peoples in struggle
in total
        Resistencia!
and with plena
        Dignidad.

                    -- *austin, tejas*
                    october 10, 1992

ON THE POLICE MURDER OF JONATHAN RODNEY

Death Dirges
        make no lilting sounds
only heavy trudging—
        as of prisoners' lonely
                shuffling feet.

Death dirges
        make no syncopating saxophonic sounds...
just mournful tones
        like tolling bells.

Hell! The stink 'n' stench
        of wanton murders,
sickly smells that tell of other
bullet-riddled corpses, sprays of lead.

Headed for the cemetery,
Seattle is somber this Sunday
as Dallas & Denver were
somber in their stead.

Dead peoples who are Black 'n' Brown
which just amounts to being down
and poor.

Doors slammed in your face
Dis/
        graces American avenues
news becomes old hat/
jive dis 'n' dat,
As we raise high the banners
torn from tattered
history pages
soaked in blood.

                —*seattle, 1978*

JESSE SILVA

My name is Jesse Silva, AKA: MR MAGIC.
I was born on March 17, 1980 in Seattle,
Washington, but was raised in the Yakima
Valley. I am a Pisces and a 17-year-old
Mexican who likes to draw, party, and
listen to music. My favorite singer is
Ramon Ayala. My values in life are peace,
love, and happiness.

LIFE

Caught in the web of violence
No place to run stuck with gunz, drive-by'z and long
nights selling that death in a pipe
Cops all in sight got in a fight
9 to his head
"Pay up" or be dead
Ya that's what I said
But POW!
Now I see the light and the flight of stairs with a pair of
Nike Cortez
Forces start to make me walk,
Talk to the rhythm of a new beat
No more heat
Now I start to seek,
Peek into the real world and the pencil is my sword.

GIRL, WHY?

I'm sitting in a state of loneliness, sadness, and darkness
since I haven't been with you.
I often take deep breaths cuz I don't know what to do.

All I have in my mind is your face with a smile, but now
that you're gone, I'm dying inside.
I have no denial.
Those oldies ringing in my ears keep reminding me when
you were here and I'm filling up with tears.
Girl, I need you in my arms so you can take away my
fears.

I pray each day that the Lord will send you my way so we
can be together 'til it's our dying day.

Baby, I'm for you and I hope you come back so I can love
you and that's a fact.

I have no intentions to push you away, but all I have is you
babe, so won't you stay?

Possibilities that run through my mind
There's no one as fine.
You're one of a kind.

I've been rolling the dice taking chances in life, but I guess
my luck ran out cuz my world been turned upside-down.
Please don't put me down.
I feel like a clown.

Ever since you been gone everything has come to me
wrong.
With a frown on my face, damn I feel out of place.

I wanted to talk to you when I was away, but I couldn't
find the words to say as long as there are stars in the sky,
I'll be with you 'til the day I die.

IT'S THE M-A-G-I-C

No this is not the land of the free.
There's a price to pay so I pray to make it to the next day.
I got the blood of an Aztec warrior.
You're better off that I told ya.
Now you know what you're dealing with.
No this is not a myth.
Don't get caught up in the mix.
Media pulling them tricks.
Life, a fix for the dope fiend.
Life's not a dream.
Don't taste like whip cream.
So I start to scream
HUELGA.
Now say strike.
Time to put up the fight.
We have you in sight
and my belt's on tight.
Time to show you what's right.
Don't take a bite of the fruit
sitting in that thousand-dollar suit.

LIKE A FLY

Like a fly that got caught,
entangled in a spider web
on the bright street light,
your black shadow
dancing in the night
with a wicked laugh
you say
you're mean.

SPIDER

My beautiful Spanish name is not important in this matter nor my sex. But I must let you know that I'm Mexican. I am twenty years young and belong to a family of eleven by blood. Things I love to do most are drawing, listening to music, trying to understand, and figure out the simple world. I was raised in Eastern Washington, and so far survived the barrio lifestyle. Thank God. Even though times look like they're getting harder, I now see the light at the end of the tunnel.

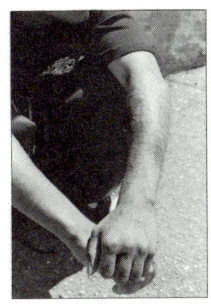

WALKING BY

Every single time that I
look into your eyes
it brings me happiness
I see our paradise

Are you the missing puzzle
to my joy and happiness?
Can you fix into my square
and relieve my loneliness?

Cuz often my feelings have
deceived and cruelly lied,
Should I give your love a chance
or just keep walking by?

MI'JO

My eyes finally opened and
I was at my terrible twos.
Mi'jo
don't touch that
'cuz the cucuy will get you.
With a blink of an eye
my age was now
eight.
I was under the church benches
mad at my padres, so full of hate.
Mi'jo
don't be mad or upset
for you are still young
and wisdom you'll get.
Rebelling, fighting I'm now fifteen
living every vato's life,
it seemed like a dream.

Mi'jo, stop!
You don't need that cuete.
But in those days you couldn't tell me nothing.
¡Hasta la muerte!
Sixteen and frozen with shock,
son, you are guilty,
the man joyfully mocked
—my eyes closed—
As my heart sank, my mother's tears fell
my padre caging his anger.
Damn your justice and to hell with your jail!
Mi'jo don't worry
everything will be okay,
just don't get in trouble
dios will show you the way.
Three years have passed
but it wasn't in vain,
'cuz I've found peace of mind
my eyes are now open again.

DEAD FLOWER

As the mist commences to rain
Beginning silent then crying with pain
You took the color and life from our blooming flower
Which in no time the earth's soil devours
I often see you in a crowd moving as if in slow motion
With glimmering dark cappuccino eyes.

ANGEL VILLALOBOS

I was born in Seatttle, Washington, July 6, 1982. I currently live in Seattle with my grandparents and my little sister. I go to Franklin High School where I'll be a sophomore in the Fall. I am an artist. My art is *mi vida*, my life, it's a way of expressing myself, my opinions, my feelings. My future plans are to continue school and hopefully attend the Seattle Art Institute. I don't know what I want to be, all I know is that I am going to be me for now and will continue just the same.

CHANGE

moving us like boulders we're soldiers
marching on
fighting for our freedom
we won't succumb
to the injustice of our nation
new creation another explanation
we're the future the wizards
the creators
a new beginning has become
are you aware of the situation
no time for relaxation
get your ass up for recreation
we are full of pride
in ourselves
you cannot hide
if you lie to me you lie to yourself
be truthful stay real
does this appeal
to the mind too sublime
in a hypnotic note
erotic quote
they criminalize the speakers
they eradicate the teachers
what'cha gonna' do when the tide comes in
if you are ready then let's begin.

LISTEN

Relatively straight
we create
time just passes
rancid like acid
disintegrate
one second too late
by a molecule
one step up
or lady luck
that's what we need
pray for the weak
the fiends and preserve
in our minds
we need to find
the meaning of life
confusion disillusion
recruitment for the war
do we adore?
Glorify the evil
like Evil Knievel
or bullwinkle
a twinkle in your eye
I spy or deny
a tear drops
do I cry?
Clouds pass me by
can I follow?
Do I need to survive
to stay alive
a soul for soul
fall into the black hole
an abyss
like a fatal kiss
we like to twist
the truth don't say
do
understand
take my hand and stand
for what you believe in.

WILD CHILD

I used to be an angry young wild child
causing trouble and chaos
filled with anger, sadness, and very confused.
So I ran away from my problems,
ran away from my family,
ran away from my home.
While I was away, I had time to think.
The angry wild child in me
broke down
and I cried.
The wild child cried.
When I returned home
The wild child calmed down,
was more caring, respectful, and understanding.
The wild child is still there
and her anger still lingers
like a taunting memory.

MY EYES

Through my eyes
I can spy
be you
see you
run and cry.
Return from the journey
new expedition
add it up like
multiple division.
Your elixer
fixer is what you need
all I can say is that you're a heroin fiend
run for cover
run from fears
all I can do is
shed bitter tears.
I've told you, scold you
reached out my hand
retold you, hold you
get up and stand
irrelevant celibate
is what you should be
I didn't ask to be born,
why did you have me?
Up in heaven
he's looking down
he's watching your every move,
look all around.
Till you realize
that there is no other
you need to know
you're an addict for a mother.